I Want to Be the Poet of Your Kneecaps

I Want to Be the Poet of Your Kneecaps

Poems of Quirky Romance

Edited by

John B. Lee

Black Moss Press
1999

©The authors Black Moss Press, 1999

Published in October, 1999 by Black Moss Press, 2450 Byng Road, Windsor, Ontario, N8W 3E8
http://www.blackmosspress.on.ca
Black Moss books are published with the assistance of the Canada Council.
Black Moss books are distributed in Canada by Firefly Books, 3680 Victoria Park Avenue, Willowdale, Ontario M2H 3K1 and in the United States by Firefly Books, P.O. Box 1338 Ellicott Station, Buffalo, New York, 14205

Canadian Cataloguing in Publication Data
Main entry under title.
   I want to be the poet of your kneecaps   an anthology of love

Poems
ISBN 0-88753-325-6

1. Love poetry, Canadian (English) Lee, John B. 1951-

PS8237.L612 1999   C813.008303543   C99-900734-3
PR9195.85.L612   1999

ACKNOWLEDGMENTS

Bartlett, Brian "Kissing in the Carwash" from Underwater Carpentry (Ekstasis Editions, 1993). Reprinted here by permission of the author. "Thanksgiving in an Old House" from Granite Erratics (Ekstasis Editions, 1997). Reprinted here by permission of the author.

Brown, Ronnie R. "Background Shadow" first appeared in Arc # 26, Spring, 1991. Reprinted here by permission of the author. "The Key" from Re Creation (Balmur Poetry Series, Ottawa, 1988). Reprinted here by permission of the author. "Old Love" first appeared in CVII, Vol. 19, #1. Summer 1996. Reprinted here by permission of the author.

"Bruck" "Julie", "The End of Travel", "Waking Up the Neighbourhood" "Perceived Threat" and "Nancy" which first appeared in Carousel, 1998 are all from The End of Travel (Brick Books, 1999). Reprinted here by permission of the author and Brick Books.

Lee, John B. "I Want to Be The Poet of Your Kneecaps" from Never Hand Me Anything If I am Walking or Standing (Black Moss Press, 1997). Reprinted by permission of the author and Black Moss Press.

Pepper, Leila "Coffee House" "The Shell Mirror" "Hearing Albeniz Tango" and "I Have Come in to Quiet Waters" from Love Poems for Several Men (Black Moss Press, 1997). Reprinted here by permission of the author and Black Moss Press.

Swede, George "The World's Greatest Blues Singer" from Tell-Tale Feathers (Fiddlehead Poetry Books, 1978). Reprinted here by permission of the author.

TABLE OF CONTENTS

Preface	John B. Lee	9
The One Who Got Away	Barry Butson	10
Dick and Jane Have Sex	Richard Stevenson	11
Men at the Shell Station	C.H. (Marty) Gervais	14
Fourteen	Hugh MacDonald	16
High School	Patricia Young	17
Coffee House	Leila Pepper	19
Flesh and Bone	Barry Dempster	20
Patient in Desperation	Barry Butson	22
Peaches	Glynn A. Leyshon	24
BackgroundShadow	Ronnie Brown	26
Sanctus	Hugh MacDonald	27
The Girl That Thomas Hardy Saw	Robert Currie	28
Local Man Weds Chicago Maiden	Eugene McNamara	29
Roundelay	John Tyndall	30
Slaves	Roger Bell	31
Skin-Aesthesia	John Tyndall	32
Love You 'Til I Die	Hugh MacDonald	33
Hearing Albeniz's Tango	Leila Pepper	33
The Shell Mirror	Leila Pepper	34
Coupling	Gary Hyland	36
Love Poem	Hugh MacDonald	37
Kissing in the Car Wash	Brian Bartlett	38
Long Term Occasional: Midriff	Noah Leznoff	40
Performance Anxiety	Noah Leznoff	41
Homebodies	Barry Dempster	42
Mavety Street	Bruce Meyer	44
I Think About You When I'm Wearing Silk Underwear	John Tyndall	45
Your Large Nose Etcetera	Karen Mulhallen	46
Animus	Penn Kemp	47
Cousin	April Bulmer	48
The Poetry Club	April Bulmer	48
Sour Grapes, Sweet Mango	Penn Kemp	49
Sex Next Door	Julie Bruck	50

The Mysteries of Sex	Steven Michael Berzensky	51
The Most Creative Act	Robert Currie	52
I Have the Power	Lea Harper	53
Adjustments	George Swede	54
To the Sculptor	James Reaney	55
Sex Is Like Geological Time	Patricia Young	57
The Lake in July	Lea Harper	59
Waking up the Neighbourhood	Julie Bruck	60
Last Night	Robert Currie	61
Diane Dances	John Tyndall	62
Kissing the Dancer	Robert Sward	63
Dance	Roger Bell	64
The Key	Ronnie Brown	65
My Muse	Robert Sward	66
What To Think By The Side of the Road	Marty Gervais	67
You'll Never Know	Eugene McNamara	68
You Weren't Here When You Were Away	John B. Lee	69
Crossing Boundaries	Bob Hill	70
I Stopped Writing About You	Marty Gervais	71
Arriving By Train	Robert Hilles	73
Marriage	Bob Hill	77
My Wife Waters the Flowers	Barry Butson	78
Fall in the Garden	Ronnie Brown	78
Thanksgiving in an Old House	Brian Bartlett	80
My Wife's Closet	Barry Dempster	82
Advent	April Bulmer	84
Heartland	Eugene McNamara	85
Oozing	Barry Dempster	87
For Margaret	Eugene McNamara	88
Vasectomy	Richard Stevenson	89
In and Out of Light	Robert Hilles	91
The World's Greatest Blues Singer	George Swede	94
Poem for Tanya	Steven Michael Berzensky	95

Ghazals VII, XIV, XVII, XXIII	Judith Fitzgerald	96
Never Buy Too Much Life Insurance	John B. Lee	98
House For Sale	George Swede	99
A Place to Keep My Words	Robert Hilles	100
The Stirring of Notes	Brian Bartlett	102
The Marriage Bed	Laurie Smith	103
untitled haiku	Richard Harrison	103
Fundamentals of Poetry	Marty Gervais	104
Is There a Better Time (Than This)?	Barry Butson	108
Centrefold from UBC	Noah Leznoff	109
Ann Noids	Richard Stevenson	110
In the Evening	Robert Currie	112
Melting	Steven Michael Berzensky	113
Truce	Steven Michael Berzensky	114
Perceived Threat	Julie Bruck	115
Freya, Norse Goddess of Love	April Bulmer	115
Love in the Middle Ages	Penn Kemp	116
Nancy	Julie Bruck	117
My Computer Sleeping: A Lullaby	Bruce Meyer	118
Dr. Yu	Noah Leznoff	119
Conjunctions	Bruce Meyer	121
The Doctor's Notes	Gary Hyland	122
One for the Road	Robert Sward	124
Poem Based on a Conversation with a Black-eyed Goalie in a Hockey Dressing Room	John B. Lee	124
Ya Gotta Know Yr CanLit	Al Purdy	126
Old Love	Ronnie Brown	128
I Have Come in to Quiet Waters	Leila Pepper	129
The Wait	George Swede	130
Medonte Hills	Roger Bell	131

I want to be the poet of your kneecaps. To call them out like an archae-ologist gently brushing earth from a curve of painted crockery. A thou-sand year old preciousness he might hold in his palm saying, "this is the reason I am alive. I exist to rescue the ages residing at your bend-ing legs."

I want to be a poet of your ankles. Those rosebuds closed above your feet on either side. To say there is a promise blooming in the bone, a sweetheart's secret pressed forever in that book of flesh.

I want to be a poet of your elbows. A poet of your inner wrist where the pulse is trapped and tapping out the quickening code of love. A poet of your chin and brow. The one who worships at the temple by your hair.

I would be the poet of the nape of your neck. I would be the poet of toes. I would linger, musing on the neat fiveness of your hands. The tiny divot of your philtrum. The creases of your ears. Surely the blueness of the iris is pool enough for some, but what of the pupil, black as a circle of felt on a false poppy.

Yes, there are certain obvious flowers of longing, but I would be the poet of difficult desire. Let me celebrate the slight plumpness of the belly about the navel.

Let me be the words connecting your luminous cable to the stars.

THE ONE THAT GOT AWAY

Barry Butson

> *"She was just seventeen*
> *if you know what I mean."*

yeah, she was beautiful
and rich and from away over
on the other side of the river
and jesus she actually liked me
sent her friend as emissary
to me at the home form brush party:-
"Janne is crying   She wants to go home with you."
imagine
she wanted to ride in my dad's old Dodge

so I agreed and she found one too
and off we went back to the city
full-out to properly scare them
show respect for who we were
drinking Cincinnati Cream we'd bought
at the bootlegger's for the first time, shaking

We parked by the river   (my side)
and just talked and laughed
about things you laugh at in the spring
when school is almost over
and you know damn well your world and hers
will never   never   never   touch tongues

DICK AND JANE HAVE SEX

Richard Stevenson

Dick wants Jane. Jane wants Dick. They want it. Uh, uh, uh.

Dick lives with his Mom and Dad. Jane lives with hers. The trick is for Dick to find a way Jane can come out to play.
The trick is for Dick to find a place. Look, Dick, look.
Jane does not like brambles up her ass. Where can Dick and Jane be alone? Where can they be comfortable for the time it takes?

Dick drives a '55 Austin A-50 sedan. It is all he can afford. Too bad, Dick. It's too difficult here, even with the doors open. Dick and Jane know. They've tried it here before. In the front seat is a big steering wheel. The three-on-the-tree stick shift always gooses Dick. Uh, uh,uh. The back seat? Too narrow. Jane puts one big leg up on the back seat. One big leg up on the front. Still no good. Dick's Tyrannosaurus Rex arms scrunch up against his chest. Dick cannot fondle Jane's breasts

See Dick sigh. Sigh, Dick, sigh. See Jane look up at the sky. Look, Jane, look.

Now Spring has come. Dick and Jane can walk the dog. Come, Spot, come. Wag, wag, wag. Dick has found a lovely glade. A hogfuel path where joggers run. Run, Spot, run. Doggies do their business here. Watch your step, Dick. Watch your step, Jane. Hurry up, Spot.

Dick ties Spot to a tree. Stay, Spot, stay.

"I love you," Dick says, and Jane takes off her panties. "I love you too," Jane says, and Dick pulls out a safe.
Together Dick and Jane put Dick's safe on baby Dick. Baby Dick sits up straight. Stay, Dick, stay. Dick squeezes the air out of the nipple reservoir. This act reminds Jane of putting up wallpaper. No. Of burping the Tupperware before putting leftovers back in the fridge. Ick, ick, ick.

Eventually, the logistics are taken care of. Dick kisses Jane. Kiss, kiss, kiss. A couple of Gouramis. Dick sticks to Jane. Jane sticks to Dick. Dick fondles one of Jane's breasts. Fondle, fondle, fondle. Dick is paraplegic, trying to strengthen his grip. Jane's breast is a rubber ball.

Dick licks Jane's breast. Dick licks the other breast.

Around the aureoles goes his tongue. Round and round each nipple equally. Now this one, now that one. In smaller and smaller circles. Just like a tether ball, getting closer and closer to the pole. Oh, oh, oh. Now his tongue has wrapped around this one. Now it has wrapped around that one. Now a playful nibble. For this one and that one.

Hard nipples, like maraschino cherries. Mmm good.

Jane for her part licks Dick's ears. Dap, dap, dap, goes her sweet little tongue. Just like a finishing brush around the delicately fluted molding of each one. Her pointed little tongue probes. Now inside his ear, now out. Jane is painting the window of Dick's soul and doesn't want to miss a spot. Her breath is hot on Dick's skin.

So hot Dick moves on. Follows Jane's lead. Pretty soon he is painting her tummy in long even strokes. Moves his tongue up and down her tummy. And daps at her belly button.

Tee hee hee.

Oh, oh, oh, Jane groans, and rocks from bun to bun to get more comfortable. Dap, dap, dap, goes Dick's tongue. Now along her hip bones. Carefully round her pubis. Slowly, carefully, probing lower. Parting the hairs of her brush like a little boy hunting golf balls. Deeper and deeper, probing the cleft of her mons. Deeper, parting the lips of her vagina. In and out and up, until Dick's nose is rubbing her pubic bone. And now like Spot in his dinner bowl.

Round and round. Up to his ears in pleasure. Rooting, rooting for her clitoris. Spot chasing a gopher far down a hole as his nose will go.

Until his tongue gets tired. Until Dick decides it's time. And Jane guides baby Dick like the nozzle of a hose into the gopher hole. To chase the gopher out some other orifice maybe. Her every aching pore perhaps. And Dick feeds himself to Jane, inch by slow inch, easing his glans over the lip of some mysterious well. Dropping the bucket of his will inside her, hand over hand. And Jane arches her back and cups Dick's buttocks to take all of him inside her. And Dick humps Jane. Hump, Dick, hump.

And Dick's buttocks glisten in the moonlight. "Oh, oh, oh," Jane moans. "Uh, uh, uh," Dick grunts. "Ooo, ooo, ooo," Spot whimpers. Spot is not having fun. Spot wants to play too.

See Spot lurch See Spot strain at the leash. His face just like Dick's. Big carotids bulging. "Ooo, ooo, ooo."

"Oh! Oh! Oh!" Jane exclaims in falsetto accompaniment.

"Uh, uh, uh," Dick replies in rut, thrusting his proud penis home. Hump, Dick, hump. Uh – uh – wha-? What's this? Strange titillation. The feathery flick of canine tongue between his buttocks. Oh! Oh no! Dick cannot come. Jane sounds like a record. First on 78. Then like someone pulled the plug.

No, Spot, no! Don't hump Dick! Get up, Dick! Quick! Stay, Spot, stay! Baby Dick's gone droopish. Suffers post nasal drip. Dick still wants Jane Jane still wants Dick. Spot just grins.

Grin, Spot, grin.

THE MEN AT THE SHELL STATION

C. H. (Marty) Gervais

It was late fall
and I would see the men
at the back of
the Shell Station
—a dim light of
the garage interior
the men sitting
on wooden milk crates
borrowed from the
dairy across the
road – playing
poker, a brand
new '58 Monarch
on a hoist like
a prize stallion
and me and my
buddies outside
going around the
back to climb atop
a mound of
discarded tires
and oil drums
to crouch
at a broken window
and listen to
the same old
stories, mostly
talk about women—
never their wives
mostly friends'
wives – horny
little things who
couldn't control
themselves
And we'd glance
at one another

fearing our own
mother's name
might be mentioned
but it never was
and we wouldn't
have known what
to do if it was—
our brains stirring
with secrets, imagining
things that made
no sense to kids
barely 12, and
after a while
our hands and
feet were freezing
and we'd climb
down in the
darkness and
we'd stand in the
street, someone
would light up
a crumpled cigarette
scrounged from
some dad's
pocket and
we'd take turns
smoking it
and marvel
at the rings
rising miraculously
in the cold
fall air

FOURTEEN

Hugh MacDonald

She and I were walking
and we came
to the stump of an elm
in a clearing
and beside it
a clump of burdocks
and she went
to the stump
which was damp
and covered
in black slime mould
and she sat there
talking to me
as if she didn't care
about her skirt
as if she didn't know
I could hardly speak
because of how she looks
in that sweater
my whole body
growing numb
and I'm afraid
to look her in the eye
because she'll know
what's happening inside me.

High School

Patricia Young

For months I've been traveling the distance—
from my basement homeroom to his third floor locker.
Walking down the hall from Typing to Algebra
a girl can only guess at the laws of nature.

From my basement homeroom to his third floor locker
I see him out the corner of my eye.
A girl can only guess at the laws of nature,
why a boy would bang his head against a metal door.

I can see him out the corner of my eye.
On all sides, combination locks dangle like plums.
There he goes now, banging his head against a metal door.
The day, like any other, is an open mathematical sentence.

On all sides, combination locks dangle like plums.
At noon there's the more practical problem—where to stand?
The day, like any other, is an open mathematical sentence.
Outside the principal's office we smear ourselves against a wall.

At noon there's the more practical problem—where to stand?
I gag on potato chips, he speaks German nonsense.
Outside the principal's office we smear ourselves against a wall.
It's a kind of geometric transformation—

one gagging on potato chips, the other speaking German nonsense.
All afternoon the brick school is a dark hive humming.
It's a kind of geometric transformation.
At three o'clock he buzzes down the banister.

All afternoon the brick school is a dark hive humming.
I can feel an equation take root in my body.
At three o'clock he buzzes down the banister.
How can we know that love is mostly ridiculous?

I can feel an equation take root in my body.
In the school library, he pulls a book off a shelf and pretends to read.
How can we know that love is mostly ridiculous?
The sun beats back the clouds so I stand in front of the window, blocking his light.

In the school library, he pulls a book off a shelf and pretends to read.
Our teachers have much on their plates but ours are empty as a Friday afternoon.
The sun beats back the clouds so I stand in front of the window, blocking his light.
The bashing thing he does with his head, is it a mating ritual?

Our teachers have much on their plates but ours are empty as a Friday afternoon.
This morning, walking down the hall from Typing to Algebra, I wondered:
the bashing thing he does with his head, is it a mating ritual?
For months I've been traveling, traveling the distance.

COFFEE HOUSE

Leila Pepper

O to be young again
to have long hair to toss back
to move with the music
small breasts thrust out
throat tight with song
to be part of them all
swaying like lilies in
the breeze of their youth
arrogant   proud-bearing   beautiful!
unaware of how swiftly
it all passes

FLESH AND BONE

Barry Dempster

We could see her coming round corners,
the only girl in high school
with swiveling breasts, those
squeezed red sweaters
bleeding the rest of her achingly
white, fantasy
drawing crooked lines
in my unworthy chest. How often
the hallways crowded me against her,
my elbow disappearing into her flesh
like doubting Thomas' trembling hand.
Inner peace soft as a sofa, the high-backed
kind, perfect to hide behind, to
bury in. One red touch, one dream
come true, and I could live the rest of my life
holy, a limestone bed.

She even had a knack for swivelling
into my prayers, just as I was about to ask
for world peace. No use being reverent, she
simply sashayed into my head, trailing
her fingers over all my needs, filling
me with the crackle of burning cellophane.

Opening my eyes, surrendering, my body
one blink away from joy, the prayer
invisible again, the world still
shooting itself in the foot.

God made stars, hydrangeas and breasts, such
was my furiously spiritual logic, a
why not hobbling through my soul
on crayon crutches. Amazing images
of running on my knees towards her,
exploding on impact, only one of us
crawling away. A small price to pay

for love. Hungrier for flesh
than for heaven: a million volts of lust.

But the Brethren had a thing or two
to say about desire, folding it up
and sticking it in napkin rings. One day
there'll be a wedding feast, kisses light
as angel food cake, flesh floating to God.
Any other appetite came crisp from hell,
a pair of torches burning down the world's
corners, exposing a boy
to his deadly bones. Slowly, slowly,
sex consumed you, your spirit crying out
just once as it spilled to the ground.

And so, she walked right past me, her
breasts aimed for a left turn
at the end of the hall. My heart
rolled back in place, tombstone and
all. For years I prayed with
my eyes propped open, nothing but light,
an empty head bowed over an empty bed.
Only sound asleep, dreaming lower
than right or wrong, did she ever
let me touch her, my hand plunging
beyond words. Kneeling in an endless
hallway, oh Lord, oh God, the world
as round as my overflowing fingers.

Patient in Desperation

Barry Butson

They drove you crazy when the time stood still—cruising in pink
time and you could wear any hat you like, pants were narrow,
draped, and cuffed, girls wore bare legs under skirts, and
we cruised around and around because
you never knew what might be there
the next time—even then, we were
patient in desperation.

We had money for smokes and pool,
interested only in who had who,
what openings were available
and when would our break come?
Patient in desperation.

Hair greased and shaped, shoes suede and brushed, ready to dance, but
afraid to ask, eager to perform, but
unable to play, wanting to grow, but
straying below, motors revving but
wheels spinning...patient in desperation.

Heroes all around us: hustlers
on dance floors and in pool halls,
heroes who were heartless and beyond pain,
no girl could reduce their manhood with a no
or resist their inclination for long.
See them dance where do they learn it?
Watch them walk her off the floor,
arm around her and big big smile.
Whose son was that who could be so cool?
Not my mother's   not yours either.
So we just had to be
patient in desperation.
In school or hockey we could skate rings
around them, but knew it didn't count,
no matter how warmly adults assured us
of our future greenings. The time was now,

stood so still, and they were the ones scoring,
not us...   we were just   patient in desperation.

So Easter petals came and went, cars
bumped, teachers taught, farmers farmed,
girls got pregnant and mothers cried.
Kings died or just got tired
and spot dances were announced
nearly every Saturday night at Teen/20.
But all we did was eat fish n chips,
swig real Pepsi Cola, and pray
that all that grease
that held us down would someday
release us   to be born anew
as great white knights
purposeful in armour
pure pink in sunsets

and it did.

Peaches

Glynn A. Leyshon

Peaches he called her
for her small breasts,
full and firm,
ripe and bursting with
the juices of life
and the name suited.
Fine and sweet
soft and tender,
with velvet lips
and ember eyes
hot and haunting
wreathing up like smoke
into his dreams
with visions of those moments
of magic, and fruit
of guile and deceit,
made all the sweeter
somehow, and spent,
guiltless, thundering
with blood, engulfed
completely in a satiation
of all the senses.
Words superfluous
they communed by
emotion, high and electric
unable to speak
to describe what
consumed them both
in those moments
plucked and chosen
with delicacy and care
savouring, rolling
on tongues of lust
and love.
Peaches do not last
delicate. Sweet as they are,

ephemeral, easily bruised
a moment of pleasure
then gone, gone
as lightly
as a falling blossom.
He should have known
that Peaches
would leave a taste
he could not forget.

Background Shadow

Ronnie R. Brown

Behind me
cool, cool
lips on the nape
of a summer's evening
leaning toward night
leaning, tongue
delicately licking salt
from the rim
of collar bone
unexpected,
a secret
Valentine in the mail,
            kiss
under mistletoe.
Behind me
and I could be
anyone—female, male, all
lovers—anything
readied, positioned to
leapfrog, hearts
bolting like Greyhound
bus revving up, shifting into me
and I could be
anywhere, years
from that breath
so hot on my back
porch,   so hot
I cannot
leave it
behind.

SANCTUS

Hugh MacDonald

I remember: the open censer,
charcoal
glows white hot,
two silver spoons of incense
sprinkled,
clouds form
         and lift:
Et introibo ad altare dei
Ad deum qui laetificat
juventutem meum
air alive with angels,
         sunbeams charged with dust.
Dandelions, buttercups,
black-eyed susan,
daisy and lilac,
the dancing stars
on the green harbour,
a baseball card
held by a clothespin
purrs like a cardboard cat
across bicycle spokes.
Twelve years old.
The fine hair
on the back of my neck
teased by passing wind.
Everything under the sun
or the moon whispers
one girl's name.
I am in love
with Linda's hazel eyes...

THE GIRL THAT THOMAS HARDY SAW

Robert Currie

> I think if we had met
> At any other time
> I'd not be troubled by it yet
> Or caught in pantomime.

> But meeting much too late
> And stranded face to face
> I wanted much to celebrate
> Though frozen in my place.

> I was quite lost because
> You stopped and stood so near
> And then emotion like applause
> Brought silence to my ear.

> You meant to speak, perhaps,
> And wondered what to say
> While out of breath and near collapse
> I smiled and smiled away.

> Oh, weird and wild is love.
> It holds a person fast,
> Or one it ought to give a shove
> It leaves alone at last.

Local Man Weds Chicago Maiden

Eugene McNamara

from *The Berwyn Life*, 1952

The wild enraged swan
that chased my wife up
a hill when she was a
child didn't get her but
I did—

That year in Berwyn Park
I sat with my father
watching semipro ball had
peanuts no salt stale as
the summer air—

The train went past up
on the embankment hurtling
silver going who the hell
knew where we were all
still back there in the
bleachers—

The swan went where swans
go my wife grew up her
big eyes bigger than when
she ran up a hill into
my arms oh my dear I said
my heart frantic as wings—

Roundelay

John Tyndall

I want to taste your hair
your long hair
the hair that flows
over your neck
your pulse-warm neck
the neck that leads
to your ear lobes
your naked ear lobes
the ear lobes that mimic
both your nipples
your softly hard nipples
the nipples that echo
off your cleft
your sweet cleft
the cleft that beckons
me to taste your hair

SLAVES

Roger Bell

As the eavestroughs brim the mosquitoes say yessssszzzz, at the midnight screens they long and they drone, they throng they moan yessssszzzz, slaves to desire

the air is too small to hold it all as you, premenstrual prisoner to a moon gripped in the soaked sponge of clouds, as you lean across the bed the room shrinks to a gasp you push your mouth a dark bruise against the lesser dark of midnight and drag your breasts' heavy fruit the veins blue and bursting against the pale translucent skin, brush the please hard nipples across my chest so breath fails my lungs slow beneath your longing crush, my lips ache to kiss the air and my hand finds those other lips which under gently turn sweet and slippery swell to the music of the mosquitoes who approve, who lean into the screens, their lives in the balance and ours glide as cars pulse past, their tires in the unrequited wishing for the wishing for the wishing for the road sounds, the melt and rise of steam into a surcharged night, and inside their internal combusting hearts the oil runs hot and fierce and says to itself less viscous less viscous pump and push of pistons' swish wish

and the gutters can't take it they think they can't take it, so full the roof trusses groan and the heavy ground can't soak up one more drop, when the skies open and the rain really rains and the mock orange bush just outside the listening window soaks the air with its tongueheavy syrup and the ditches course in the simultaneous mutter and gush or our yessssszzzz

and the mosquitoes applaud and batter their keen shoulders against the fine strain of the mesh and you, you turn to me your eyes unsettled your heart still uneased your legs open up and my pores expand to take it all in, no I can't but I can't, but the mosquitoes say yessssszzzz slaves they are they say yessssszzzz we are slaves they sing blood they sing again to all this fecundity, this desire, they say yes yes yes yes yes

SKIN-AESTHESIA

John Tyndall

This is our ritual
holy connection
my hands my fingers
your undraped torso
whereupon we transform
the colours of warmth
the music of touch
listen as ripples ring
around ocean skin
my wild wind
your tidal moon
all the scents
of cricket choirs
all the tastes
of low loon call
we feel together

HEARING ALBENIZ'S TANGO
Leila Pepper

At my age
I should be ashamed
to remember
my mind should be
on Last Things
repentance   salvation
     and what comes after
but today I burn
I remember your eyes
I remember your mouth
not what you said but
how you looked at me
your arms would be
salvation
I repent nothing.
Yet — how quickly
it all passed!

LOVE YOU 'TIL I DIE
Hugh MacDonald

I love those moments
when your praying mantis
body craves nutrition
and I am victim
and victor in one.
You lie there
smiling in your sleep
and I your willing servant
come tender
to your bed.

THE SHELL MIRROR

Leila Pepper

When he died
I gave away everything
but a worn tweed jacket
hidden in his closet
      and the shell mirror

Get rid of it
throw it away
it will only bring pain
they said of the mirror
lying on my dresser
It is a ring of sea-shells
spiraling periwinkles
glued awkwardly around
a base of shiny foil
when you stare into it
it reflects a crooked image
a tiny distorted face
a kindergarten child
could have made it
but it was carefully crafted
by my husband   at Dayaway
our mutual respite

I remember my fear
the first time he went there
he walked away from me
down the path hand-in-hand
with his driver   then turned
to wave good-bye   and I
felt the same emptiness
I had when our eldest left me
for school years and years ago
Coming home hours later
he told me in a worried whisper
there were old women

who couldn't talk!
Sickies I'd call them
he didn't see himself
ravaged by Alzheimer's

Time moves strangely
those old men and women
in short days were his friends
co-workers and buddies
and he was happy because
he was needed
he belonged

in remembering that terrible time
there is pain
one can't forget it
but I remember better how he loved me
and that the mirror
my crooked beautiful mirror
was his last gift of love

COUPLING

Gary Hyland

Some mornings you wake up
and you're not there.

Who is this who taps your
wife's butt, struggles

to the kitchen for coffee?
Not last night's stud

of mad Casanovian
innovation

inspired by wine and a snug
mid-winter storm.

This is the one whose night
of high passion

is to snore through three
new videos,

the guy who each week day
slogs out the door

to do repeatedly what he
does, then does more,

who drives one of four routes
never other.

Give him an engraved plate.
But you want grapes

placed neatly on her navel to
slowly nibble,

lubricious hot-tub massages
under candles

with sultry enticements
thickly whispered.

That the two of you cohabit
confounds your wife

but shouldn't since she and
Ms. Betty Blah

baffle you blind by sharing
body and brain.

Betty, Queen of the chronic
fatigue shinbone

who yawns while I caress
her stubbly leg.

How can this matchless pair of
pairs love and thrive?

The trick always is to mate
couple and date.

LOVE POEM
Hugh MacDonald

I remember hands and mouth on you
round breasts so full
moist sweet pearls
drop gently on my chest
sensations touch and drift away
a snowflake in a witch's cauldron
stirred by a melting stick.

KISSING IN THE CARWASH

Brian Bartlett

Sometimes light dims,
the onslaught of things
drives us from the wind

and the window
to each other's eyes. Forces
shake senselessly, we

can do nothing
to stop them. It's a liquid
world, awash with

fateful shapes
blundering
mechanically,

where we come to rest
like deep-sea divers
chained, our oxygen

running out.
For oxygen, good oxygen
my mouth goes straight

for yours, and it's a liquid
world, fuller than summer's
peak, the industrial thud

slowly fading
in our own lush wash
closer than home. We overlap,

more than over-
lap, we lap, we taste
good to each other, so

steal my breath, lickety-
split. My better lips, my
lap, you banish

all dross—
precious simplifier...
complicator.

Back in the hard glare
my sight runs and leaps
thanks to your sight,

to my tongue's
dark red memories
of your tongue,

your close whisper louder
than the heedless waves
flooding around us.

LONG TERM OCCASIONAL: MIDRIFF

Noah Leznoff

something new from the mud of love
something growing in the fingers
something like the something I almost saw today
something like the 320-pound technician
  like the bookshelf
  like rainwater rushing to the sewer
  like the child dizzy in my arms
  like the last smoke – and I mean the last one
  or the aboriginal e-flat in a wine bottle
something like rehearsing for death
like the intestinal bight
like today's TV massacre of the week
or the joy we wish for in moments of absent mindedness
  something the gift-giver wants

  something like cinnamon
a red sky, seven lean years
the embarrassed tough guy
or the girl in math class who, fingering her
jean button, laughed
  leaning back and low in her chair, bucking slightly
for the circle
of boys magnetized around her:
  "Let's play a game and see who can give me
    the most compliments; I'll keep score til the end
    of the month!"

  or the silent boy who shouted from across
the room

PERFORMANCE ANXIETY

Noah Leznoff

> "They make their nests of clay, one mouthful at a time."
> —from *The Wonder of Canadian Birds*
>
> or
>
> "How you make love is how God will receive you.
> —Rumi

making love I can't shut out the train
in my head:

    will she come, will she come?
    is she coming, will she come?
    will she come, is she coming, will she come?

or
how will this next touch
occasion love, that more or less generous
everything—

a full salad of kisses seeming
to ride on this humming—
bird wing,
this distance-sustaining pendency
through sugar-carrying wood
between trunk and
flower; this red

heart whirring at eighty vibrations per second;
heart coming, ruby -throated, to slough its own name;
red heart a birdly engine or blooded machine

But Christ, we've been friend enough to beauty, you
and me, to friendship – take your hand from my
mouth, say it:
        talk is good
        empathy is good

books and film good good
humour, honesty, volleyball, food
good good good good

no, say it now diving into me
the flat of your hands against my chest,
we'll say it together
as laughter
    nothing makes love like *rumba*.

HOMEBODIES
Barry Dempster

The trigger-happy Parisian desk clerk makes it trés clear
that not one corner
of his bleary hôtel is home.
The black hole of the stairwell
does not take lightly
to our book of matches.
The shower head
is dripping something green
and the bed is yellowed
like old newsprint ghosts.
And the view, toilet pipes
and sweaty brick, not even a TV
to entice us with its colours.
Hardly romantic, the kind of
ambiance where fucking
is more adjective than verb.
Oh city of dinge, where we
embrace in desperation.

Remember our foreplay in
Miami, the room smelling
like cold cellophane.

My tongue almost freezing
to your air-conditioned nipples.
An entire night of longing
for extra blankets
the furry kind that leave
stubble burns on the cheek.
And then Ireland, that house
of peat, where the dampness
leaked between the sheets
every move we made
a squelch.

I've been heartbroken in many
countries, sex fleeing like a cockroach
startled by the light.
No wonder it's the young
and elderly who travel most
soft knapsacks and reclining
tour bus seats.
While the rest of us homebodies
curl up with thermostats
in one hand, TV remotes in the other
leaving just our tongues free
ecstatically familiar.

MAVETY STREET

Bruce Meyer

for Kerry

When moonlight stole like guilty cats
        and summer owned the air
I kissed your lips on Mavety Street
        and tousled your starlit hair.

Grave windows on the darkened rows,
        the abandoned dairy's shell
cast off their grimy prose of life
        and wished two lovers well.

The old men in the Balkan Hall
        looked up from losing hands—
my love I pledged on Mavety Street,
        more heart than head or glands.

Your tiny flat was heaven's realm,
        the roof leaked sylvan streams,
but you and me together there
        was daylight to my dreams.

And moonlight stole the years away
        and summers drank the air,
I thirst for that kiss on Mavety Street
        and the starlight in your hair.

I Think About You When I'm Wearing Silk Underwear

John Tyndall

I think about you
wearing silk underwear

I hear the fabric rustle
like autumn leaves
in offshore winds

I see the colours iridesce
like hummingbird feathers
at flowery sip

I feel the weave slip
like rain-water
through my fingers

I smell the mossy fragrance
like a déjeuner sur l'herbe
in the bedroom

I taste the dampness
like a distillation
of pure nectar

I think about us
wearing silk underwear

YOUR LARGE NOSE ETCETERA
after e e cummings

Karen Mulhallen

My friend georgie didn't
want to poke her nose etcetera
in etcetera but during my recent
love affair could and what is more
did
tell me just what a
love affair was

for
my brother sam thought
that all English men were
etcetera and made scores
etcetera and scores of etcetera
telephone calls not to mention
surprise visits invitations
since he knows
just what a love affair
my sister sue hoped that
I'd emerge
intact of course and
knew that I'd know
just what I'd been missing
mean

while I
was home alone
lying
in my bed etcetera
thinking of your eyes, crooked
teeth, smile
jokes, large
nose etcetera

and everybody knows
just what a big Nose
is good for.

ANIMUS

Penn Kemp

eye
I am
I am mew
I amulet
I am you lettuce
I am you let us be
I am you let us be wit
I am you let us be witch
I am you let us be with Chuck
I am you let us be with Chuck cling
I am you let us be with chuckling grace

I am you us
and a muss
anonymous

Cousin
April Bulmer

She doesn't see very good; she got a eye thing. It's like spiders
in the blue part. It's like when the moon draws itself over the
sun.

When Cousin and me go out, I hold her in the crook of her arm and I tell her
when to step down and I tell her when the sprinkler's going to spit and I tell
her the light says green.

And sometimes we go out for a coffee. She takes hers black so I
don't tell about the sugar and about the pitcher of cream. We like
to sit at the booth in the back cause we got secrets. Cousin's got
a big voice and she laughs deep, but I know there is a cry in her,
it's wet and runs wide like a puddle. There is a cry in me too.

Today on the way back, a man on the bus, he got big sad eyes. His
shirt got a print of wild birds: ostriches in stride, woodpeckers:
their beaks. A sparrow's nest. He makes a gun with his finger and
points it at the puff or red feathers where the heart beats. I
don't tell Cousin about the man. And I don't tell about the
robin's tender breast.

The Pastry Chef
April Bulmer

And in the batter of my dreams your breasts rose round as biscuits: two mounds
of sweet dough warm under a tea towel and my touch.
The crust on your nipples I softened with lard and washed away with milk.
You were of late wheat and the blessings of bakers and priests.

SOUR GRAPES, SWEET MANGO
Penn Kemp

I will give you hands to cup
our birth; I will open my mouth
for your words to spout; I will
sew your seeds for pumpkin to sprout.

I will tell your midden on you.
Lost glove, lost love, soggy
in the puddle of repentance.

I will mother your vinegar.
I will press expression from
your store of gripe; I will
stomp cepage out of first fruit.

I will nurse your trees and
branch your feral diagrams
till fair grounds down to humous
on the old playing field.

O apple of my eye, impeach me,
I am impaired and chary.

I will rant till the rave's over,
dawn's done and eve's nigh
coming. I will remonstrate,
demonstrate, set you straight.

I will spell you right and left.
I will formulate, articulate, initiate,
even ingratiate as long as I am
not too late to utter attention.

Attention, please.

SEX NEXT DOOR
Julie Bruck

It's rare, slow as a creaking of oars,
and she is so frail and short of breath
on the street, the stairs–tiny, Lilliputian,
one wonders how they do it.
So, wakened by the shifting of their bed nudging
our shared wall as a boat rubs its pilings,
I want it to continue, before her awful
hollow coughing fit begins. And when
they stop to have (always), until it passes, let
us praise that resumed rhythm, no more than a twitch
really, of our common floorboards. And how
he's waited for her before pushing off
in their rusted vessel, bailing when they have to,
but moving out anyway, across the black water.

The Mysteries of Sex
Steven Michael Berzensky

Today, after he reads yesterday's newspaper
in the Laundromat around the corner, he trudges home
through the glaring snow, carrying his clean clothes
and the expropriated paper. The stairs creak.

to his basement room. On his bed he marks and clips
articles for folders he has labelled ALL ABOUT DREAMS,
THE WORLD AND ITS ABSURDITIES, THE MYSTERIES OF SEX,
LEISURE TIME AND UNEMPLOYMENT, OLD AGE & DEATH.

When he is through clipping, he deposits the folders
inside his old army surplus steel suspension filing cabinet.
He makes himself supper. Between four slices
of eighty percent whole wheat bread he spreds

some chunky peanut butter and orange marmalade.
Then, one can of Vegetarian Vegetable soup (condensed)
to which he adds a half can of tap water, heated up
a thick broth. For dessert: a cold spartan apple.

After this, a hot shower. He stands in the steaming
stall for half an hour, beads of fervent water,
streams of torrid air massaging his back.
The green bar of soap, which smells somewhat

like cinammon, diminishes to a sliver
before it softly slips down the drain.
Then, the highlight of his social season.
He and his latest fling go out to a movie

at the theatre downtown. Afterwards, they ride
the city bus to his favourite pizza parlour.
They share a cheese and anchovies pizza.
Her share: one-eighth. His: seven-eighths.
For conversation they discuss THE WORLD AND ITS ABSURDITIES,
LEISURE TIME AND UNEMPLOYMENT, THE MYSTERIES OF SEX

After pizza, he walks with her to the bus stop.
They wait in the falling snow. They stand apart.

He: Maybe we should've had a plain pizza
She: No. I adore anchovies.
She steps inside the Number Five bus,
is swallowed by the warm light.

They wave good-bye. Why could he not obtain
even a goodnight kiss? The bus churns from the curb.
Strangers bundle past. He is standing alone
in the falling snow beside a street lamp.

The crystals slanting down resemble commas.
Periods. Semi-colons. Question marks.
But mostly, they resemble asterisks. Those
miniature six-pointed stars that land and dissolve

on his heavy frayed overcoat. Those soft footnotes
plummeting from the sky. He feels like one of them.
Tumbling continually. Never clinging. Melting
into the fine colourless composition of the night.

THE MOST CREATIVE ACT

Robert Currie

He thinks of counterpoint the
cadence of a catalectic line that breaks
another curving back upon itself   the flow
into caesura's calm   texture
of vowels and consonants   expect
ations dashed the stretch of
tension   aesthetic   distance.

He sets himself the task:
write the poem   and   never
mention her smile.

I HAVE THE POWER
Lea Harper

It's a matter of alignment you say
as you pass through the wall
not magic
but frequency
Brushing the atoms from you
like plaster
you slip into me
I believe you
I am a woman
I have the power of opening
You however must cup your hands in prayer
match resonance with the right mantra
with something other than chance
(Flattery is known to help
That's how the Red Sea parted)

No one disappears into thin air
They just live beside us
in other songs

You reach under the hood of my pelvis
like Houdini's last attempt
at something there is no way out of

ADJUSTMENTS

George Swede

(The first year)

He wants her
to be like his
maiden aunt
and tend him
with care
like a
delicate plant

She wants him
to be
something else
of course—
a lion
of a man
or at least
a horse

(Ten years later)

She inspects
his leaves
with love
every day
and he tries
to respond
with a spirited
neigh

TO THE SCULPTOR

James Reaney

All the arts present themselves–
      Words   Mouth
      Ears   Music
  Carving–the transport of touch
   The sculptor & his model:
Sometimes he falls, she in his arms,
His chisel rolls across the floor of studio
Another wedged–descending into the cave of her
He, his hands on her shoulders, feeling the push
Of his force below against his hands pushing down
    Against the soft-stiff chisel carving a child

All other arts are but caresses, hugging,
A finger in a belly button, that bricked up gate.
    This, the sculptor's art alone
       In three dimensions
    Makes flesh out of stone.
All other saviours are but surface sailors–
This gives to Thomas a wound in His side
      For his doubting finger
A wound from which a spear has shattered a stream
     Of fructifying water
Drowning the pursuing Pharaoh & his skeletons.

      Sculptor! pursuing with your sharp
   The woman hidden in the marbleblock
  Or the man, the juventus with his sling shot,
      His magic wand
     That Solomon begot.
  The rain carves a mountain
    Into populous plain.
 I feel the sun himself
Pounding us with a fiery mallet,
    Holding his dark planet in his hands
     Of dusk and dawn
   Beneath our feet tonight.

Unseen beat his golden tides
Against our daylight side
With the chisel of light he carves our whereabouts
Lost in the midst of a stone
Sealed in granite fog,
Sculptor!
With thy soft hard rod
Wheedle me out.

SEX IS LIKE GEOLOGICAL TIME

Patricia Young

People will tell you they married for love
and I've said that too but now
I'm too old for such lies. I've seen it all—
the terrible bodies slammed together in dust.
What we're made of
spins us together—churning things
that assume
a single,
disc-like shape. And when places
break off
and become planets
parts of ourselves cool in the distance.
At eighteen I crouched above him
and it was like looking
into eons of fog. I couldn't see past
my shrinking self. Or was I
expanding? And always
the hammering of meteorites, craters
being blasted out of molten
rock, oh he was a boy
with lofty ideas
but I kept rising up beside him
all water and hunger. We didn't notice
plants and animals
beginning to appear, we were too busy
sliding belly against belly.
Ah, the pact to be true.
Who were we kidding?
The body springs from the earth,
untamable as the grasses.
If I showed you things speeded up—
seas swamping deserts then draining away,
mountains erupting and wearing down,
species becoming extinct
or evolving into new forms—
you'd see what I saw

looking down
from an unmade bed, you'd see
the north and south poles
wandering like lost children
for somewhere solid to dig in their heels.

When I was young I didn't know what it meant—
I looked in his eyes and saw continents
drifting away
from a single land mass, my legs
were always buckling
beneath me, I didn't understand sex
is like geological time, and change
so gradual
you can only see it
if you look back over your shoulder.

THE LAKE IN JULY

Lea Harper

This is the day you longed for
months ago
under a blanket of snow
To close your eyes
and see the sun
streaked in waves under your lids
the shadow of your lover
crossing over
a bridge into new lands:
berries filled with blood
cedar thick with musk
his taste on your tongue

Doors flung open
your sheets set sail on twin maples
The body sheds its dying cells
for stars stolen from the night

You open your eyes
to the mauve lake
a shroud at daybreak:
the outline of the trees
the outline of your life
liquid, shimmering
like a song sent out over water

You wonder how long
the earth has been soiled
the heart this heavy

The lake accepts your tears
To her you are weightless
What isn't swallowed up
is drifting away
drowning or being born
Apart from the wind
ruffling the surface
what else actually happens?

WAKING UP THE NEIGHBOURHOOD

Julie Bruck

Just back from California this early Sunday,
and now, those introspective singer-songwriters, or Bach
even the manic genius of Glenn Gould–just won't cut it.
Outside, in the gentle, Montreal morning
of my childhood, an old man shuffles past
on the arm of his paid, young companion.
Pink impatiens do what they do in orderly beds,
as the odd cyclist zips by in black & white spandex
under Sherbrooke Street's arched maples.
A homeless man, his hand out for change, seems
tentative, almost apologetic. In San Francisco,
I heard someone tell a panhandler, "Sorry man,
but change comes from within." Yes, that's
a non sequitur, and neighbours, I'm sorry.
But this moth on the window-screen is too grey
and plain to me, after driving the fire-seared hills
of Oakland, after crossing the Bay Bridge
to the city at nightfall, as banked fog moved,
like pure violet cataclysm across the navy bay.
Neighbours, this calls for Peter Gabriel,
his over-blown synthesizers, over-laid drum tracks.
Neighbours, we live like orderly mice here
atop the Laurentian fault, pre-Cambrian
and deep as the San Andreas. Surely, this
calls for a brighter noise. I'm sorry, neighbours–
you, concert pianist; you, sleepy optician;
you, McGill Phys-ed coach with the girlfriend,
here only on weekends–I'm sorry. But the man
I love sleeps on his side in that other language
of signs, instead of what they signify. I'm sorry,
neighbours, to wake you from pleasant or anxious
dreams, but the very limestone under your beds
is grinding against itself right now (for God's
sake, I could have put on Wagner's marches!),
and this building settled on its foundations
nearly one hundred years ago and trembles
with every bus that goes by. Neighbours,
I'm sorry about all this bass and percussion
so early on a Sunday, but hey–d'you feel that?

LAST NIGHT

Robert Currie

There was laughter at the table,
music on the floor.
Though the dance brought us together,
something more held us there
where your dark eyes lit a mirror
hidden somewhere at the core.

I felt your light inside me,
knew just what you meant:
silent ships on moonless nights,
in the dark a closing door.
I hope you make the harbour,
but I'll never be with you.

A moment's not forever
though it may not be forgotten
and it wouldn't be forgiven
it must end when it is over
though it goes like the river
that's rushing by the shore.

DIANE DANCES

John Tyndall

You want to two-step
she can give you two-step
with a one two-knockout punch
you want to waltz
she can give your waltz
whirling and swirling
from here to Vienna
you want to fox-trot
she can give you fox-trot
sly step and slide
to give dogs the slip
you want to polka
toe-to-toe so fast
accordions wheeze their last
you want to jive
she can give you jive
till the boogie-woogie cows
come home to little boy blue
you want to twist
she can give you twist
you'll go up and down and
round and round and round
you want to watusi
she can give you watusi
to make peace break out
in Rwanda and Burundi
you want to slow dance
she can give you slow dance
every sway a blissful eternity
you want to dance
she can give you dance
no shadowplay on walls
but the primal fireflight
Diane Dances

KISSING THE DANCER

Robert Sward

Song is not singing,
     the snow

Dance is dancing,
     my love

On my knees, with voice
     I kiss her knees

And dance; my words are song,
     for her

I dance; I give up my words,
     learn wings instead

We fly like trees
     when they fly

To the moon. There, there are
     some now

The clouds opening, as you, as we
     are there

       Come in!

I love you, kiss your knees
       with words,
Enter you, your eyes
     your lips, like

       Lover
Of us all,

     words sweet words
     learn wings instead.

DANCE
Roger Bell

for Val

This then is marriage
as best I can tell
after twenty five years it's
rounded, like a waterworn pebble.

We sleep like spoons
nested
one gentleness, an undulation
of hair and skin
and when one stirs, and sighs
the other replies.

This then, I suppose
is marriage
the choreography of the familiar
the tender pas de deux on
the deep dark stage of night.

THE KEY

Ronnie R. Brown

for Jim

Yes, I confess
I've sometimes dreamed
of other combinations:
imagined
what a tumble (or two)
could do
for my sense
of security; at times
even thought
of breaking free.

But
useless apart,
together we
open up to
untold possibilities. Yes,
we are a pair,
a set: a well-worn lock
tripped only
by a single cut of key.
With familiar ease
you find your way in me. A flick
and we are both
              undone
have,
yet again,
come home

MY MUSE

Robert Sward

> As a rule, the power of absolutely falling in love soon vanishes...
> because the woman feels embarrassed by the spell she exercises
> over her poet-lover and repudiates it...
> —Robert Graves, The White Goddess

"Why don't you just write a poem, right now?" she says.
"'Western wind, when wilt thou blow...'
why don't you write a poem like that,
like that 'Anonymous'? Something inspirational."

"Talk about muses," I sulk,
"Yeats' wife was visited in her dreams by angels
saying, 'We have come to bring you images
for your husband's poetry.'"

"Yeah? So what?" she says. "It's out of style.
I already do too much for you."

Odalisque in a wicker chair,
book open on her lap,
dry Chardonnay at her side,
hand on a dozing, whiskered Sphinx.

"You need a muse," she says, "someone beautiful, mysterious,
some long-lost love
                    fragile, a dancer perhaps. Look at me..."

"Yeah?" I say, refilling her glass,
"You hear me complaining? You zaftig."
            "Zaftig?"
        "Firm, earthy, juicy, too," I say.

             *   *   *

"Juicy plum," I say, in bed, left hand over her head,
"rose petals," I say, right arm around her.

"Silver drop earrings," I murmur, ordering out
for gifts. "Aubergine scarf, gray cashmere cardigan."

I do this in my sleep. go shopping in my sleep.
"Oh, yeah, and a case of Chardonnay."
Wake to the scent of apple blossoms,
six decades in the glow of roselight.

*   *   *

"Wake," she whispers. I tell her my dreams.
We kiss. Poppy Express. Racy Red. Red Coral.
     Star Red.
          Red red.
I tell her my dream.
          "Enough. That's enough," she says.

WHAT TO THINK BY THE SIDE OF THE ROAD

Marty Gervais

Am I wrong headed
to think this
as the road sweeps
before me like
a checkered table
cloth you might've
spread out on the grass
for a picnic?
I shut off the
car and sit by
the side of the
road and catch the light
falling at dusk
across the fields
of newly-shorn seed
corn, a farmer
ambling across
the stubble, the

end of day–
Am I wrong headed
to think that a tired
glance, a movement
of your head, the
way you turn from
me in a room, or
in the bed
beside is a sign
of change   just
as this season ends
as this day comes
to a close?
Am I wrong headed
to believe we are
merely lovers
who unfold our limbs
separating for an
instant embrace
frantically clinging
like the last leaves
on the tree
in late October?

YOU'LL NEVER KNOW
Eugene McNamara

When my wife is away
I still sleep on my side–

If I wake in the night
her side is a big vacant
silent space like a place
where a tooth was pulled

Gently I place my tongue
in the empty place so
it won't hurt–

You Weren't Here When You Were Away

John B. Lee

My wife says this
by the pool in the summer upon my return
for I was away
within the unfixed image of myself
in the south
where heat annealed colour
brightly on the hills
by daylight seared like fire
looked at through a burning glass
and yes
I was away in the solipsism
of absence
yes, I was away
in the centuries of memory
and map inches
measured beyond the third unfold
but I thought on you
love
and I appeared beside you
where the pillow dipped
with a blink of linen
and I touched you there
with a water drop of dream's caress
that would not wake desire
though it close the stars
together whispering sparks
in an intimate astronomy
the night sky shares its galaxies
caught burning while you slept.

CROSSING BOUNDARIES

Bob Hill

I wish that I might speak a language
    that you could understand.
I would send the words across the room between us
    by a courier who, passing the barriers of time and place,
    moving beyond all signs of darkened reason,
would make you pause and listen with a clarity
    you say you've always wanted.

What I would say to you in this new hearing is
    that most things that matter–don't. Most of them–not all.
The ones that do have counted all along–moments gleaned together
    and put aside because of all their smallness
    until we have forgotten they are part of us.
And that the labour of our duty must be abandoned–cast aside,
    until only people stand to look at one another.
Each of us a host and each of us a guest,
    standing equally with the clothing of our journey about us
    and our birth and death held within our hands–

held within our opened hands as gifts to one another
    and received with a grace and gratitude
that would serve as the only kinship needed.
    Then respect would come
as it does for those who have been stripped by time
    of all the obligations
    danced to through the years.
We would speak then through all the interdicts
    with an honour that surpasses all we've known.
And if that constructs a love, then let love stand
    as speech, sufficient to itself, and wordless from the start.

I Stopped Writing About You

Marty Gervais

I stopped writing
about you.
about the days
when we sat
in a large porcelain tub
in a house with high ceilings
our bodies, as exotic flowers
unfamiliar, unafraid
our names, mysterious secrets
Sitting for hours
letting the winter darkness
envelope us
telling sweet narratives
of our lives, joys.
things that went wrong
tracing our histories
never realizing
we were making our own,
tracing out a future so full
of uncertainty, so full
of chaos, of grim
afternoons on days
when everything went
wrong, and when
we couldn't look
at one another,
yet we'd come back
to one another, in the
early morning when
I'd retreat to the bed
after a night of
insomnia and wandering
the dark house
and staring at all the
pictures, the empty
darkness, until I'd tire

of it all, and slip in
beside you
and you'd put your
arm around me,
the soft warm touch
of your hand on
my belly, and it
seemed enough
more than scrambling
for the right words

Arriving by Train

Robert Hilles

i

Reading on the train
from Jasper to Vancouver
I think of you
alone in the house
wearing my shirt
typing pages of your novel.
The one I'm reading
is not keeping my attention
and I stop often to look out
at the scenery.
I keep imagining myself
entering your office
to place my hand on your warm neck
to feel the words pulse there,
anxious for the page.
I read book after book
looking for our story,
the one that explains
how our love joins us
even when we are miles apart.
The same dull grey fall sky
nearly rubbed clear of light
covers both of us
and I want to write our story
let the details loose upon the world.
Instead I turn pages of the novel I'm reading
lose track of the plot and put ours in its place.
I am drawn to you bent over your laptop
shifting the words left or right
finding the exact place for each.

ii

Dark clouds fill the sky in the west

as if they hold night inside
and wait to slip it over the train
like a heavy wool blanket.
I think of you arriving home from work,
fixing a bowl of cereal and sitting in front
of the TV, alone.
I imagine you in one of my shirts
and I wish I were those sleeves
clinging to your skin
feeling the warm news
from your heart.
I know there are new stories
starting every day
stories like ours
never written down before
but still cluttered
in the mess of words somewhere
waiting for pages like these
as white as the snow
resting on each limb outside.

The train weaves between mountains
and from the last car
I watch the headlight vanish
and reappear up ahead
like a search light
sweeping the tree tops
out of habit.
Do you hear me
whisper I love you
in your ear as you eat your cereal?
Do you feel me watching over your shoulder
as you type more words,
as you work towards the end
as we all do,
one word at a time,
slipping them so carefully in place
that it looks to others

like they were there all along?

iii

It is completely dark now
and the moon hangs behind
a thin layer of clouds.
Now and then it hesitates
as if shy about disappearing
behind a bank of trees.
I think of moonlight descending the stairs
at our house, exploring rooms
as if looking for a place to stay.
I see it slide along your arm
and sigh in your ear.
I put my fingers
to the cold glass of the train window
and draw across the moonlight
the shape of your arm
and for a moment this is the only story
the one that gets written
over and over in all those books
the one no one can guess the ending to
the one you and I sigh into the night,
once and for all, our story,
everyone's story
the one being worked on every day
because no one
yet knows it all.

The train moans through the night
weaving back and forth
like a restless sleeper
keeping me up.
I lift the blinds at two in the morning
and look for your face in the dark
invisible mountains.
When the trains stops,

I want to get off
and call you
let the phone lines
sing my longing.
Instead I watch the train men
hunched over, walking around
in the dark like men about
to commit a crime.
One man stands against
the rail yard fence and watches
and I sense we are
each of us afraid of something
we can never quite put into words.
I stand like that man
watching him in the dark
a shadow watching a shadow
until the train moves out of the station,
and he shrinks back into the dark
as if never there at all.
I pull the shade and feel lost
in the pale interior of my sleeping cabin
the walls a dull grey-green metal
and I lie back on the bed
still missing you, knowing
each night away from you
is far too long.
I slide my fingers over the blanket
thinking of you at home
tossing aside the quilt in the night;
your pale skin
caught in the moonlight
fills my head, and I lift my hand
to draw it along your leg
to your feet, warm
and soft to my fingers.
I fall asleep like that,
my fingers between your toes,
for even in sleep I couldn't pull away.

Later I will arrive by train
my luggage dangling from my arms
and I will stand on the cold platform
my hands numb under the weight
and still I will feel my fingers
between your toes
warmed there like they belonged

MARRIAGE

Bob Hill

    It was a way they had
to sit in winter darkness and listen.
    6:00 was determined by the L&N
Usually punctual – he would check his watch
    She her supper preparation.
The whistle precipitated action,
He admired punctuality – "Right on time."
She the sound in December gloom–
    "It's so lonely, so lost out there."
Each evening passed the same with different ways of listening.
    The same sound each night – and two divergent needs
        One for order
        One for mystery

MY WIFE WATERS THE FLOWERS
Barry Butson

Holds the green hose in her hand,
the other in her petal-pusher's pocket
      lime-green nozzle spraying
fine mists over the flower beds
and wine barrels filled
with petunias

Drags the hose up to the deck
for the hanging pot of impatiens,
then threatens to water me down too
with playful flick of the hose
    Finally, she hisses at the nervous
cat, huddling by the back door, guarding
his fate

With a hose in her hand my wife
is an artist
of considerable talent and imagination
The flowers, cat and I
just love her

FALL IN THE GARDEN
Ronnie R. Brown

Almost twilight
when she calls him from the garden,
air scented with the coming fall;
far away
church bells toll.

He is kneeling
but from a distance,
her glasses on the table,
she cannot see the way

his trousers strain down,
the grunting-slow push
that brings him
to his feet.

She sees instead
a young man
hair slick with sweat,
skin earth-brown with tan.
The image,
blossoms on her cheeks, as her heart
begins to race.

That look,
on her face,
makes all the difference. The trowel
drops to the ground as he strides
toward her; takes her hand;
leads her up the stairs.

Bodies,
gritty with soil,
entwine,
more eager
than young lovers.
And everywhere the warm,
the wet, the scent
of sweat
and fresh-turned loam.

THANKSGIVING IN AN OLD HOUSE

Brian Bartlett

for Karen

This holiday is an empty stone well
encircled with rotted leaves. Fill it,
let subterranean streams rush in—

    for the fuchsia's red blossoms on the sill,
    Indonesian salad, ginger root dissolving
    in our mouths, the nearby siren crying
    how someone would save a life or a house,

for a single-cell noctiluca
massed and phosphorescent
on the ocean surface at night,

    for this house of pine planks and old brick
    newly ours, hand-hewn ceiling beams still
    telling stories of the axeman's swing,

for jumps to the unaxable,
the unphotographable, the unframable,

    for her, the blessing I never expected,
    her voice and hands, all of her, all,

for everything mating our laughter,
optimists "those who say bad weather's
better than no weather at all,"
                for wind
rubbing our faces when we climb
to a ferry's top deck, in a gannet's wake,

    for the lungs to lament, for all who curse
    a ferry's death and a monster bridge's birth,

for rain on the roof (as long as it won't
leak any more),
    for as long as, even if,
yet, still, dashes and parentheses,

    for the Anarchist who gardens
    the daycare centre in the seniors' manor,
    the keychain skeleton hanging in the hall
    and every other unlikely pairing,

for ingenuity, ingenuity!–
Hearne and his men in 1770 cutting up their tents
for shoes; Muir in Alaska, 1880, scraping shavings
from his sled, tiny kindling to brew tea,

    for all who read closely, all who read
    carelessly, (whoever slap-painted the sign
    METHODIST CEMETERY BAKE SALE)–
    for *brouhaha, dogsbody, rigmarole, bosky,*

for the bedrock that no done day can be undone,
for regret, so the next game flies fiercer,
for sleep without nightmares, the healer,
that fall into blankness from which we rise
into each other's arms like startled swimmers,

    for the mouth and fingers to give thanks
    and the Zimbabwean thumb-piano, it's mighty pluck
    ringing to all the corners of the room...

My Wife's Closet

Barry Dempster

A dim grey day until my wife
swings open her closet doors
and the room is startled with
the sheen of a thousand flowers,
dresses blossoming haphazardly,
skirts cascading from hangers
like honeysuckle blooms, blouses
bunched in shimmering bouquets.

I remember my mother's closet
with its hopscotch plaids and hushed pastels,
like a board game for Avon ladies.
A beige pair of polyester pants
rubbed up against a pink sweater
with buttons that shone like tiddlywinks.
Skirts so rough and grim they must have
been woven from clumps of widow's hair.
A blue angora sweater
shedding like a nervous Pekinese.

The closest I come to infidelity
is wondering what lurks behind
the closet doors of all my female friends.
As a child, I imagined Sandra Dee
folded perfectly
in a box lined with chiffon.
Cousin Joan running
her long, red fingernails
through a rainbow of linen and silk.
Even a stranger's face
on a rainy day, a mist of
green eyes and plum-coloured lips,
like a glimpse of doors
open just a crack.

I am often found
in my wife's closet,
which is half-mine
through marriage's giddy legality.
Fingering the surprisingly
silver roses of a party dress
I feel far beyond myself
(a mere man hanging laundry)
like Jason sealing his thumbprints
on the edges of the Golden Fleece.
And I could almost swear
this purple and scarlet
skirt of flying poppies
is more than just something
my wife likes to wear;
it's the way she dreams
when days are dim suits of armour
and frost has mussed her eyelashes
with crystals of grey air.

ADVENT

April Bulmer

We have never trimmed a Christmas tree:
hung garlands or ribbon
from fresh boughs.

Tonight, I pray God we might
walk through seasons.
Tilt together
as the earth rubs her hip
against the sun again.

For thirty years
you have written of God
and our small freedoms
and truths.

As the earth moves away
from her warmth next Advent
may we choose a tree, my love
that survives the Epiphany too.

HEARTLAND

Eugene McNamara

for Margaret

The geese in the park will not
migrate this winter–
They have forgotten how or why–

It's been months now since we
came home after thousands of
miles and two oil changes–

We kept stepping on the tracks of
Lewis and Clark and kept on crossing
the Missouri River over and over–

Have we changed at all?
There were those sheep in trucks
behind the Wranglers' Cafe in
Wyoming mildly regarding us but
what could we do for them?

We had gone high on those
mountains and came down to sweet
water and a land full of sky–

Our squeegeed windshield let the
whole prairie into our laps and
a combine harvest in the Kansas
afternoon worried at the dry field–

Far from Alberta where we left our
son and far from Jackson where we
did not buy Million Dollar Cowboy
Bar tee shirts–two regrets–

Far from spiked purple flowers
in the ditches of North Dakota
where sloughs crowded the road's
edge and the sky was wide awake–

If tomorrow comes and I wake to
find you next to me I'll know I am
home–

If tomorrow never comes again well
we've been there and back again–

You are the country I will never ever
fly from like geese in the park close
to home you are the map of far places
home in my heart–

Oozing

Barry Dempster

The man in the moon
gives one of those wry romantic grins,
but my wife is sneezing.
She collapses on the bed
Kleenex spread across her face
a Cleopatra wilt.
No amount of Mantovani
will budge her tonight.
Her body belongs to the common cold
an ancient cult
arising from clammy silverware
and coughing crowds.
The germs oppose her
liquefying her very will.

The dark forces of biology
dog me day and night
my DNA as limp as
something on a microscopic slide.
And now my wife oozing
right before my eyes.
The cat on my lap
sweet and fuzzy
is rippling with bacteria
as surely as the damp patches
down my basement walls
the yeast in my slippers
the microorganisms
on my fresh fillet of sole.

The Doukhobors had it wrong
when they praised the inner light.
Wiser, the neurotics
who know every pore
is a tiny abyss
amoebas glistening

like funeral candles.
I creep closer to my wife on the bed,
unable to control myself.
No virus ever looked lovelier.
Just a kiss, a subtle bite
the moon going green
as graveyard grass
diseases colliding with a squish.

FOR MARGARET

Eugene McNamara

I wake to the dark and
stare at my dream going
up through the roof and
look for the room's stretched
walls my eyes could not
follow

You are deep in your own
dream in a place I can
never come to

Now my eyes are friendly
with the dark   the walls
are there again as usual
and I can just make out
the known shape of your
face so near to me closer
than my own or my dream

I sink back into dark
and dream of a country
where I am wholly known
the way you know me
in the noon of common day

Vasectomy

Richard Stevenson

The decision was simple enough.
Sex isn't some funny uncle from Desmoines
who talks your ear off about plumbing
fixtures and valves, or harrumphs and egads
his way through hot tips of insider trading
while he puffs away at his dimestore cigar.

You can't console it with a back rub
or dusty old tin of Copenhagen snuff—
even if it promises you candy
or a shiny new silver dollar
for going to the store for it.

You are not a piggy bank
and it can't fill you up that way.

Nor is your body a parking meter
that can take pills like endless
rolls of quarters, and always be there
when you want to go out dancing.

We cannot expect lightning bolts from heaven
to light up the main circuit panel
then travel down the line
to some copper key kited high
inside your uterus either—
not without blasting the tree
to its very roots.

Love is not a shooting gallery.
There is no one to yell "pull,"
no guarantee every clay pigeon
will be hit by a perfect bullet,
even now when I plan on shooting blanks.
The target is not something you hit or miss.
You were not made from Adam's

or anyone's rib, as the fused halves
of my glans, the line up
the shaft of my penis show.

The decision was simple,
something we could even be glib about:
it's easier to work on outside plumbing
than chase a knotted bit of cloth
with a snake throughout your pipes.

Just as we turn off inside taps
so the water in the outside faucets won't freeze
and burst the pipes behind the drywall,
this little precaution with my spigot
may steal a little juice from Peter
so we might afford to pay Paul.

Or say we are tending our garden, love—
pruning suckers from last year's roses
so they continue to bloom with promises.
Though our children grow apace,
we can find the garden again.
We need only tag a branch,
to find our old initials
still growing with the tree.

In and Out of Light

Robert Hilles

In and out of light we touch
finding where each body
continues from the other.
All week I haven't slept right
and have awakened in the night
to you there and not there.
Last night I woke every hour
counting them out in my head
my thoughts a dumb numb clock.
I woke you when I went downstairs
and I felt your anger
in my stomach all night.
Each passing car had its headlights off
as if the dead were driving
and for half an hour I stood
by the darkened window
thinking of you sleeping
in a blanket of anger across the hall.
My fingers felt along the window sill
hoping to find some way to let the anger
out of our house for good.
I wanted to throw open the windows
in the dead of winter
and let a Siberian cold
freeze it to the walls and floors.

Yesterday morning I stroked you for an hour
and felt so close
my body seemed a continuation of yours
not joined at the ribs but at the heart
here in this house
in the middle of the block
in the centre of an ordinary city.
And yet what wanders these rooms
has never been before
nor ever will be again.

It is totally ours
to mend or ruin.

I wanted to stand outside your office door
and listen to your breath,
to cross the room and fill it
with intimate details for your dreams,
but I didn't want to wake you again
so I stayed at the window
searching the night sky for some hint of the moon.
There was none.
Finally, I crawled back to bed
hollowed out my side
and felt over now and then
to yours, empty,
drawing my cold hand
up and down the length
as if you were still lying there.
And I could not stop searching
though I knew my hands would come away vacant.
I fell asleep like that, waking to
the odd noise night leaves unexplained.
You were so quiet when you left
that I woke later
thinking you must have slept in.
I rushed to your office
found you gone, the bed freshly made.
All morning I wandered the house
looking for traces of you
fearing that you had vanished
from my life for good.

In the tree outside the window
a lone magpie flitted from limb to limb
acting as if winter were an ache
it could leave behind
one branch at a time.
Its restlessness troubled me.

I felt its fear through the window
as it hunted for food cautious of danger
the mute air around it tingling with cold.
Finally it flew away to some other tree
down the street
its tiny heart pounding out the day
much like mine
carrying me one drum beat at a time
towards you, your own heart
answering across town
both of us filling the air
beat after beat.

True, this is a conciliatory poem.
I admit it.
On the table are flowers
and candles and one of your favourite meals
and this poem, white sheets flat
on the green table
yet each word is rounded
full of love
each vowel an ache in the mouth.

THE WORLD'S GREATEST BLUES SINGER

George Swede

I put it on
for the first time
since that night

why should it matter now
I had bought it for her
besides
paid good money for
the special two-disc set of
    Bessie Smith
    The World's Greatest Blues Singer

    gee
    but it's hard
    to love someone

she begins
the words
spreading through me
like a poison

    when that someone
    don't love you

making my body ache
and burn

I push
  reject

record player arm rises
like a scorpion's tail

Poem for Tanya

Steven Michael Berzensky

Tanya, now that you've left me
will you say I was gentle
and with feathery fingers
touched your face
our last day
on my bed of down?

Tanya, now that you've
left me, will you say
a winged shadow
fluttered around your body
and stroked you soft and warm?

Tanya,
now that you've left me, will you say
I was the sparrow that flew away?

Vancouver, 1967

GHAZALS

Judith Fitzgerald

Death to this book or fuck this book and fuck this marriage. Fuck the twenty-six letters of my cowardice. Fuck you for breaking the mirror...Fuck marriage and the-ology...Fuck the idolatry of anger...

—Leonard Cohen, *Death to this Book*

VII

A marriage. A room with a view.
I love you. I love you. You do.
You showed the way to the desert,
your little house, perfect records.
Assumption. Absolutely love.
In this life with you so cornered.
Mama right. Daddy sing the tune.
King of the road and the horses.
Red sky from off towards the hurt
tonight: Something about forget...

XIV

Nothing visible prepares us
for the wounds we accumulate.
Magnificent devastation
of the selves we cannot allow.
Whose eyes compare to one not there
in the middle of night's crisis?
Vernal moon supine, reclining
in velvet folds and marbling hands.
I want you stripped to gruesome. Show
the scars, the half-notes, the self snuff.

XVII

Engaged in the afterlife, stars
circle ice-blue gone moon-blanched night.
In memory sumptuous dark,
night hyacinth, heavy with it.
So utterly romantic –gone
missing –just when you need it most.
A locket and a clanking kiss:
Latches holding your heart just so.
The resentment seething, scathing.
Man, it makes you want to snuff it.

XXIII

Man, missing you with abandon.
Each grey corner reveals an edge.
Spinning in the open breezeway,
flaxen web of light transforming.
You learn to deal with envy when
you'd rather forgive the ego.
Regardless of the flesh, the blood–
Exquisitely most perfect love.
Pain, she very small – she very
small – she never feeling better.

Never Buy Too Much Life Insurance

John B. Lee

you'll tempt your wives to greedy grief
invite the widow in
wearing weeds
weeping away the black week
with one wet eye on the money
you'll murder yourself
in perpetuity
the bank notes fluttering after
tickering down
like a lovely moonlit snow
much sad singing "quelle domage
il nege, it snows"
you'll dig yourself a golden grave
see how the coin
comes shivering down
how sunlight molts like a sick fish
and me with my two penny eyes
a cheapskate's poker ante
one coppery blink away from forever.

Know this
I love you
even to the very Hitchcock music
sawing at the door
even to the dark wing
ravening at the window
even to the very knives and poisons
of your secret heart
see how I sign
and freely purchase one future
one long and seamless cruise
without me.

HOUSE FOR SALE

George Swede

Our marriage
won't fly

It walks
the rooms
peeping

Wings
tightly
tucked

Finally,
we throw it
from a window

It falls
flutters
and then
soars

Every evening
it returns
to the elm

To sing

So everyone
tells us

A Place to Keep My Words

Robert Hilles

When I returned from Vancouver
you gave me a notebook
encased in a cover
you crafted by hand.
With two different colours of nail enamel,
you drew a woman's back and hips
and then traced I Love You
with your finger.
Another place to keep your words, you said
and I lay it on my desk
where I look at the cover
and see that beauty spreads outward
from what we keep inside.
I see that your hand was steady
as you traced the words without doubt
and I've never felt so loved before.
You praise me to others
and I want to praise you too
to show the world how tenderly you smooth
your hands over me
touching me so spontaneously
I hold my breath
not wanting to let anything out.
Then you lean down
and whisper in my ear
something stored in words
and I reach for the book
to write them down
to hold them on the page
until I wander across them later
pondering what is written
while I think of you mixing
nail polish
silver and gold
to form a new colour,
one made just for me.

You draw lines down the cover;
some lines don't intersect
other lines do
and I trace those lines
fingers meeting where they cross
like ours in the night suddenly
as if from the brow of a dream.

When the book is full
I will slide it next to the others
on my bookshelf
but will take it out now and then
to re-read,
finding each time
a different past
to return to
one nestled gently
in an odd string of words.
And in all that assemblage,
I hope our love will stand out
like the single rose in a bed of weeds.
Until then, I am humbled,
and can do nothing but
fill pages with purposeful words.

The Stirring of Notes

Brian Bartlett

for Karen

In my broken-spined jotting book
  old phrases slept for years, fragments
    curled into themselves:

delice de Bouddha/Buddha's delight from the menu
    in the window of a Japanese restaurant
    smiled emptily until tonight
    when it found a fullness in you

caterpillars everywhere–under a tree,
    thick in the air like thoughts of you
    falling onto my shirt sleeves

breathing suddenly heard on a string-quartet CD–
    how could I know that such release, breath
    exhaled when one violin paused
    before another resumed, would be you?

    even lone words–
hypaethral (roofless)–
    open into you, where other planets slip through
    like the night we sprawled on our backs
    in an island's grass and hawkweed

Tonight before you secretly made
your way to the desk, then lowered your arms
down onto my shoulders, your mouth
onto my ear,
              that notebook was a forest
where anything hibernating
awakened your footfall.

THE MARRIAGE BED

Laurie Smith

I don't need all the bed;
queen-sized has become
insulting, now I leave clean laundry
folded, piled, need to put away,
my two robes (winter and summer) draped
over the foot of the
his side

an extra blanket, almost too warm,
just bundled, like
a wall at the back, a spoon
and when my dog sneaks up the stairs at 4 a.m.,
curls on the other pillow,
there is life breathing comfort
of sorts, company head to toe,
six-foot-one of mass
and I sleep well

*the haiku to which my 3 year-old daughter
condensed Walt Disney's Beauty & the Beast
when, later, we acted out the parts*

UNTITLED HAIKU

Richard Harrison

I want to marry
you. I want to touch you
with a knife.

FUNDAMENTALS OF POETRY

Marty Gervais

I was a kid
maybe 17
a copy boy
at the Globe and Mail
when I met Vern
—a hack operating
the wire service
in a back office
He'd rant on
about giving up on
poetry, saying it
was all bullshit
I could never find
the right words to defend
myself or poetry
One night he started drinking
and picked up a prostitute
downtown, brought
her in and told me
to come back
and sit next to her
How do you do Ma'am?
Vern roared, What
the hell d'you mean, 'Ma'am?'
Look at her She's
a whore!
I smiled—just
out of school
and there were no
prostitutes in Bracebridge
except the woman
next door in the show
and she was a bit slow
and we all thought
we were doing her
a favour anyway

so I just smiled
 Vern finally got up
to leave, announced
he was going
across the street
to the hotel – he'd
be in Room 217
and if New York called
I had better
fetch him, drag him
our of bed and back
to the Globe
Don't take 'NO!'
for an answer, d'you
understand? wagging
a finger at me
Things were going well
until his boss telephoned
–I told them Vern had
gone out for a coffee
and I'd get him
I bolted across King Street
to the King Eddy
and knocked on the door
Get the Jesus out of here!
he roared from
the room...I pleaded
C'mon Vern! New York's on the phone!
I could hear the springs
on the bed and a bottle
rolling across the hardwood
floors and a lamp crash
Are you okay, Vern?
Vern's voice again–
I told you to get the
Jesus out of here!
Finally, I tried the door
and it opened

There – naked
from the waist
down, wearing only
an undershirt and
black socks was Vern
–bulbous belly and all –
hanging upside
down over the edge
of the bed
struggling to reach
the overturned bottle
of Canadian Club
Get the living shit out
of here boy!
I nodded to the hooker
Hello Ma'am!
I'd never seen a
grown woman naked
except for my mother
when I walked in
on her bath by
accident one fall day
after we had moved
to Bracebridge
and like that day
in the fall, I averted
my eyes
I stared down
at Vern's shoes
in the corner
C'mon Vern, New York's
wanting you on the phone!
Let's go!
He peered up at me
–a kid lost
in a grocery store
and started in–Okay, you
want to be a bloody

poet! Well write about this!
Gesturing flamboyantly
to the room
to a picture of Custer's
Last Stand over the
bed – Wordsworth might've
written – 'Fair star of evening,
Splendour of the West, Star
of my country! on the horizon's
brink' Then whack!

Slapping the woman's
rump as she rolled
over and yelped
and rolled over smiling
at me, Yeah, write
me a poem and I'll give
you a blow job!
I was lost for words
–I'd never heard
the term, and I'd
never had one,
and as I escorted a raging
Vern back to the paper
all I could do was
think about it, conjuring
up its clinical image
I was in a daze
and couldn't write a word
to save my soul–her
red hair dazzling in
the bare light bulb light
of the room across
the street, the room
stinking of liquor
and smoke and sweat,
and that night
I rode the streetcar home
eager to learn more
about this guy
Wordsworth

Is There a Better Time (Than This)?

Barry Butson

German-blonde, she had the name and size to go with it.
Eyes cruel blue, parchment white skin and a swimmer's shoulders.

The first thing she removed was her blouse, button by button.
I've seen shorter winters.

Then she kicked off her running shoes and one by one pulled
off her socks, stuffing them into the shoes. Germanic neatness.

Shorts next or brassiere? The only question in the world
I wanted answered.

It was the shorts she unzipped from hips still slim, and in
pants and bra she looked at me like I was lunch and I was

ready to serve myself up to whatever her mouth desired.
She removed the bra to unload heavy breasts that fell an inch

then bounced, nipples so happy to be free they rose like dogs
when a car comes along. So pale those nipples and softer

than a foreskin. when she bent to remove her panties, the breasts
fell forward like coke cans in a dispenser and I instinctively

from my position on the bed turned my hand upward.
Her thumbs hooked her panties and her back bent as she stepped

out of them, her triangle of hair a little darker than blonde.
Naked, she walked over, pulled back the covers and hopped in.

A woman undressing is always worth a few words.

Centerfold from UBC
Noah Leznoff

Affection comes easily to the innocent.
                    —Penthouse Magazine

A nude, fallen backwards
   on the divan (okay, water bed,
folds of red satin), traces
 the natural
science of her nipple,
like reverie, sensual wonder,
(intense, brooding, open-mouthed
 full under airbrush, the play-light dapple
blush, apple peach pear
    split fruit
and an overturned book,
 her other finger nestled in
its spine;

upside-
 down the title reads

   The Phaedrus.

Her pride, the blood-muscle she makes,
the maple leaf, and pearl comets coming. On radio,
CBC, she's as fat with allusion
as undergrad poetry:
"I'm kathartic," and she rattles, professorial,
stats from Denmark. (I imagine her adjusting
  Hakim opticals; she is nude but
  for them – O Radio!)

And she wants
unions for sex-trade workers –a fair shake
   for the shuddering, pension plans, occupational

safety, a youth diversion programme,
      the universals.

   On pragmatism: "Plato held apart his polity
and poetry. Nothing down smooth for philosopher
things; tepid erotica for the literate
middle classes, but, God no,
don't let the masses get their hands
on the good stuff!"

ANN NOIDS
Richard Stevenson

I have this friend I met in grade two.
He's a federal government tax specialist now,
bust people who file false income tax claims.
It's a steady job; he's a steady sort of guy,
though his first wife left him to join a commune.

He's into a second home and new mortgage now,
and though life isn't exactly The Donna Reid Show,
he chugs along; pays his taxes, mows his lawn.
Some might say his life is contained by the ever-
decreasing perimeter of each swath, but so what.

He has come to this pass honestly enough.
Didn't so much grow tired of debauchery,
as debauchery grew tired of him. Cost him too much
playing the fool. Drinking and doping isn't the same
without the libido and hair. He outlived the props.

We all do, like comic strip characters he once drew:
Ann Noids, who suffered terminal post nasal drip;
Juicy, the class fat kid; Mith Patht Parithipple,
Jimmy Wingnut, the Vice-P with two tufts of hair,
Cosmo, who worked out a formula for the McDonald's log

and set about to supply the grid of ordinate
and abscissa as a backdrop to our youth–
even Coitus Interruptus, the beast with two backs
who slipped a disk in the back seat of his car,
and Fast Eddy Bangshaft, who used baggies when he

had no condom or airs left to put on. Survived
pimples, Donna Reid, the Beave, even Bela Lugosi.
And my friend was right: we were all outsized somehow:
had big ears or big noses, big boobs or balls,
and tried to mop the halls with them –

As if all these sensory apparati could somehow
move of their own accord like delicate snails
performing arabesques over the leaf mold
and filigree of all the autumn leaves,
and leave us free to smell the roses.

Survived Friday and Saturday nights too.
Paid dares to dance with Strawberry Fields, who
had pimples on top of her pimples. All the Ann Noids,
sang froid. So cool we nearly froze
in our pecker tracks, pointing the way good dogs do.

Or did we? Only our hairdressers know for sure.
But next summer's our twentieth high school re-union,
and we'll all get a chance to see outside the frames.
Myself, I'm going to keep an eye out for Ann Noids.
My guess is she's divorced. I bet she's beautiful too.

In the Evening

Robert Currie

He takes his coffee black, no sugar.
Sits across the table from the TV,
grumps at the supper-time news.
If Edna were back, he'd tell her
where the Premier could cut taxes,
why the Jays aren't winning.
Edna will not be back again,
and he is glad it's over. Was over
two years before he'd admit it,
both of them knowing the whole time.
He's fifty-six years old this month,
content with things as they are.

He reads more than he's ever read,
non-fiction, mainly, biography, history,
notices a lot about the birds. Awakens,
often, to the distant clack, clack-clack
of magpies on the edge of town. Pauses
in his gold game to watch jackrabbits
bounce across the fairway, gazes
at burrowing owls in the fourth rough.
There are wonders everywhere.
Whenever he wants to,
he takes an evening walk, follows
the Wakamow trail through the valley,
inhales air green as poplar leaves.

Tonight he sits on a bench by the river,
watches a long V in the water,
a mother mallard leading seven chicks.
In the brush something snaps. Quackquackquack.
Chics panic, kick, splash,
skitter before their mother
who paddles past them, herds
them to shore where they huddle

in gently swaying bulrushes.

A woman walks from the willows.
"Sorry. Stepped on a dead branch.
May I join you?" she asks.
Her voice, he thinks her voice
is the sound of a rainbow.
"Yes," he says, "yes. Please do."

MELTING

Steven Michael Berzensky

To feel the soft earth beneath my feet
the give and take of grass
dream of lovers in other places
see the snows vanish
into the hardness of dead seasons
was not easy for me
until you and I rolled
into a snowball
down the white hillside of my bed
into one another, into lovers everywhere.

TRUCE

Steven Michael Berzensky

Once I longed to hear
the soft chatter of your feet
across the bedroom floor.

Now we've both chosen solitude
over love and its
perpetual state of war.

Neither of us
bothers knocking
on the other's heart anymore.

Perceived Threat

Julie Bruck

I am the odourless gas seeping up from the cellar to fold
you and your children in my arms and take you down.

I am the car that comes from nowhere, just as your dog
recognizes the dog across the street and runs for it.

I am every interruption between here and there, every
dreaded phone-call, leak in your heart, snag in your stocking.

I am your sensitive tooth, the worn enamel, the nerve.
I am the woman with her elbows on your kitchen table

across from the man you love and want to trust.
The three of us are eating nachos. He leans forward.

Freya, Norse Goddess of Love

April Bulmer

Sometimes we rested beneath the winter sun: he offered me praise and hymns.
I pressed myself against the old ache of his body, kissed the blood and sea salt
from his lips. I emptied myself into his dreams and his helmet shifted as he
slept.

But one day he sailed and he would not worship, nor call upon me in the cold
hull of his ship. He rocked against the hard bones of his vessel but would not
love me in the damp night air.

I remembered the coarse weave of his garments, his thick braids of hair...his rit-
ual prayers and sacrifice under a full-horned moon.

One day I laid down and the sun made a shadow of me: against the tablet of
earth I am a scar: a rune.

LOVE IN THE MIDDLE AGES

Penn Kemp

                         This pair
are wanting teeth. Do they
chew or eschew?

                         Choose or
be determined, that is fate
accompanied. This last fairy
chose and look what she got:

a grotto of sleep, a needle in
the sack, hey, what else but
country matters matter at
sixteen going on a hundred
winks an eye and all's lost

but not departed, to be or–
nery, no snore in the whole
company come again another

sentry resistance's low why
fight the absurd. Fall back to
sleep and poem may rise yet.

Baited or not, we can be caught.

NANCY

Julie Bruck

We'd argue that night, there'd been tears, and as the car pulled out,
the only sounds were our seat-belt tongues, clicking into their holders.

Then a shout, and a dapper man in a good suit, probably sixty-five,
ran over, one hand high and spoke into his tiny, folding phone:

Nancy, I've found a space, just drive around the corner,
look left, I'm here—I'm holding it. and you, always the patient,

kind one, always quick to laugh, just drove away form how
his face lit that patch of claimed asphalt, expecting her Camry.

And I drove away with you, unable to look, convinced
that Nancy was breaking the speed-limit in the other direction,

heading for uncharted neighbourhoods in her luxury car, her
small, veined hands clamped to the wheel, that even if the man

stood there all night, punching numbers into the phone, Nancy
had other plans, Nancy was our of here, Nancy had gone downtown.

My Computer Sleeping: A Lullaby

Bruce Meyer

Hush-a-bye you diode pile.
Save your screen, make Daddy smile.
Leave the busy world to fret,
dream of sites on the Internet.

Dream of servers and CD ROM,
a place for you in every home
'til darkness passes and you are freed
by soft commandings gently keyed.

Guardian angels stand by you
that surge protectors may be true.
Let all your circuits wake up bright
guided by watts and mega bite.

Pray your user is your friend,
that every warranty may extend
another year before you meet
a future that makes you obsolete.

Dr. Yu

Noah Leznoff

Dr. Yu, you are so
beautiful it's im-
possible
for me not to erotocize
pain,
masquerading,
your eyes above the surgical
 mask; what with us nose
to nose in this
 inch-intimate business,
you must know I'm crazy
 (nudging small implication
modesty fluttering)
for this digging under
the nerves of me,
 your small brown
hands in my mouth.

We've mad pleasantries
of our children
and again I've almost
told you
a hundred times in
that minute that
your skin—
 that I need
no anaesthetic, just
a full-grown mind
and
you
Yu

See? My tongue trebles
over under everything
and the viscera
you bring me

to the tissue
of
lets me learn what's
endurable
(this
feels too much like love).

"Tell me if I'm hurting you."

Okay:
what kills is this:
willing down
in the raised-up
    tilted-back chair
a navel-kissing Viking
that would give the ship
unequivocally,
smiling, away–

that would arch in
the layered air
like a soldier under
a blanket hovering
   for a kiss,
like a heliotrope
in the day-broken
 garden after a long,
warm night of rain.

But in your book
it's likely only
equanimity & hardons
that separate aesthetes
from creeps –matters,
in the last,
   of Form.

Only

a fool opens his mouth
to his dentist
   his ache-making dentist
   married dentist
   fully classified and profes-
   sional dentist—
minute and austere and capable

in endless exquisite ways
 of saying "Buzz off

jerk!" and really making
 the point.

CONJUNCTIONS

Bruce Meyer

for Kerry

The parts of speech rattle through our lives,
the fret of prepositions driving us to do,
the nouns we wear as husbands and wives,
and verbs which live on after us as you

flip through the pages of dusty albums—
what became of us so quickly, how time flies.
What is it holds us together as the seasons
disappear like earnings and each garden dies?

Let me find you in the grammar of desire,
let me touch you in those dark hours when
there are no words, only hopes, when the fire
that cannot be quenched says begin again,

and the syntax that drives our being forms
like frost on a window pane, so beautifully,
so silently, drawing us and tracing patterns—
with, yet, and – this joining for all eternity.

The Doctor's Notes
Gary Hyland

Physical

Droops most days
like a sun-dazed snake
between two stones

Blind but highly responsive
to tactile & cortical stimuli

Ardently craves workouts
achieves few

Hydraulics semi-clogged
unpredictable
the golden bow
now a messy splurge

Psychological

Identity ambivalent
responds to various
names   Tommy Tentpeg
Peter Pointer Crooked Dirk
Shazam   Captain Poker
& What Have We Here

Lengthy depressions
brief manic sessions

Erratic attention-getting
behaviours, some inept
some ill-considered

Perks up when
acknowledged

Plagued by
inarticulate longings

Isolation-induced neurosis
    fear of blemishes
    fear of blades
    sporadic stage fright
    and mild attacks
    of impostor syndrome
    with dread of exposure

Tendency to act impulsively
on slight provocation

Susceptible to falling
indiscriminately
thus often inappropriately
in love

Treatment

More companionship
and emotional support
preferably by SO
but should take
whatever comes

Regular exercise
Psychotherapy
For aplomb
a placebo

One for the Road

Robert Sward

One for the road.
A little detached it was, but bouncy, flouncy, hoochie coochie,
woo wah woo, out there under the stars,
woo wah woo,
one for the road, one for the road it was,
and end of the show.
Stupid shit, how was I to know?
One for the road and end of the show?
So good-humoured it was, I missed the clue,
hugging and kissing, all that
hugging and kissing.
Missed just how all over it really was.

Poem Based on a Conversation with a Black-eyed Goalie in a Hockey Dressing Room

John B. Lee

He is her live-in boyfriend.
Last week she'd hit him
in the face with a pan
and so Frank says
"the flap jacks
resembled him the next day"
and I imagine them
peeled up by spatulas like wheat-flour death masks.
And this week
she'd punched him twice
in the eye...
his theory, "she's testing
to find out whether I'll be abusive"
meaning: will he ever hit back
and although he laughs
he means every word
and I imagine
a magazine list:

"Ten things to try if you suspect
your new boyfriend
might be a hitter"
a *Chatelaine* quiz involving
when to use knives
involving, the smoking gun as a last resort
the burning pillow
the small dark pin-feathered hole in a sleeper's head
where he dreams one silver bullet
and he seems so peaceful
when he's dead
and "he never struck me once,"
she said.
"Not even when I stabbed him
in the night.
He must have really loved me."

Little wonder
that he cringes for a kiss.
And they're "thinking of having kids
                together."

Years later, all his children resemble rumpled skillets
and he's the proud father
saying, "the night you were conceived, boys
            I didn't see it coming"
as he shows his sons
the slight relief of his skull repeated
as a warning
in a gallery of pans.

Ya Gotta Know Yr Canlit

Al Purdy

I'm in bed sick as hell
from sulfa drugs I'm allergic to
and this young guy phones
says his mother was Gwen MacEwen.
I say that's nice and so what?
He says weren't you a friend of hers?
I shyly admit that is more or less true
but say I'm sick in bed and may not recover
in time for funeral or baptism ceremonies
So he gets on his knees on the phone
and begs me for an interview
but jumping kitcheraboo I am dying
therefore keep your wife and maw-in-law
in the goddam car please gawd
So he drives out to A-burg
locks his wife and maw in the car
comes and sits on the edge of my bed
of pain and says he found Gwen's name
on papers at the hospital where he was born
now he and wife and maw-in-law
are on their way to Mtl. to meet paw
and paw's loving wife he married since Gwen
I say "You figger he'll take you in his arms
crying out like some guy in the King James
'Lo he that was lost now is found Hallelujah'
(or words to that effect) and the guy's wife
too will welcome the famous poet's son–Huh!"
I say "Huh?" Even at this distance form Mtl.
I can see the guy's wife's expression change
"You wanta be known as MacEwen's son huh?"
(and he does look kinda like Gwen})
At this point I'm sick enough to throw up
so he gets a wash basin from the kitchen
and holds it while I lose my innards
with appropriate stomach music
kinda going KAW KAW KAW like a lovesick crow

then "Go away please" I say whiningly "Go away"
So off he drives to Mtl. with entourage
to receive paw's prodigal son blessing
and paw's wife's immediate affection
which goes to prove genealogy is interesting
if you don't get too far ahead or behind yourself

After my guests' departure I am reading
Edwin Muir's Essays and come across
a lovely line from John Milton:
"Those thoughts that wander through eternity"
and the line soothes me like a hospital
bedpan when you're in desperate need
better'n antibiotics and about that place
where I expect to wander soon
but not yet not just yet
Huh?

OLD LOVE

Ronnie R. Brown

Days go by before you find the nerve
to check the local directory.
Vacationing in the home town
of an old love, you tell yourself
that more than thirty years
have passed. Surely, he's moved
on, out. But there
beneath his family's listing,
the one still etched in your memory,
his name, complete with the Jr.
he used to hate.

It takes restraint, but you do not call.
What would you say to him,
your husband, his wife,
the collective families?

Still, you can't forget. Roaming
the town, seeing the sights,
you seek out familiar-looking men;
hope you'll run into him accidentally.

You're almost home before you realize
that in the museums, the malls, of that quaint
tourist town you'd searched for him
among the crowds of lean, young men.

You smile, hoping–although you know
the chance of it is slim–that somewhere
in the cities you once called home, old loves
wander the streets, scanning groups
of laughing, long-haired girls
longing for a glimpse
of the one who once
was you.

I Have Come in to Quiet Waters

Leila Pepper

I have come into quiet waters
the raging sea subsides.
Far far ahead the future
like a boat in calmness rides.
My shallow craft is beaten,
Tiller nor sheet nor mast
will ever pull in wind again
for the fighting days are past.
Land-locked in the room of memory
I shall sit still and apart
though I hear the blast of thunder
shake roof and wall and heart.
But oh, will I ever remember
in some lost and dream-dim way
remember in gravest wonder,
how violent lightning shook me
how the lightning that was you
brightened and blinded me that day?

THE WAIT

George Swede

The face
a calendar
with lines drawn
through the dates

The eyes
inset windows
that show twisted limbs
across a faded-white sky

The memory
full of perfect
little moments
that fall and whirl

Then, at last, love
turns up the walk–
the steps cautious
the hips aching